# The Little
# of Talk

### by Judith Dancer
### Illustrations by Marion Lindsay

**LITTLE BOOKS WITH BIG IDEAS**

Featherstone Education
An imprint of Bloomsbury Publishing Plc

50 Bedford Square
London
WC1B 3DP
UK

1385 Broadway
New York
NY 10018
USA

www.bloomsbury.com
Bloomsbury is a registered trademark of Bloomsbury Publishing Plc

First published 2016

British Library Cataloguing-in-Publication Data
A catalogue record for this book is available from the British Library.

ISBN:
PB 978-1-4729-3038-5
ePDF 978-1-4729-3039-2

Library of Congress Cataloging-in-Publication Data
A catalog record for this book is available from the Library of Congress.

3 5 7 9 10 8 6 4 2

Printed and bound in India by Replika Press Pvt. Ltd.

This book is produced using paper that is made from wood grown in managed,
sustainable forests. It is natural, renewable and recyclable. The logging and
manufacturing processes conform to the environmental regulations of the country of origin.

**To view more of our titles please visit
www.bloomsbury.com**

# Contents

Introduction                                                    4
The role of the adult                                           5
Key principles                                                  5
How to use this book                                            7
Building vocabulary through dialogic book-sharing              9
Further reading                                                10
Activities and experiences: Indoors                            12
All about me                                                   12
Spot the Dog                                                   14
No hiding place                                                16
Little me                                                      18
Read all about it!                                             20
Any old iron?                                                  22
Kim's Game                                                     24
Tiny treasure                                                  28
A box of delights                                              30
Tell me a story                                                32
We're all going on a summer holiday                           34
Gruffalo magic                                                 36
What's next?                                                   38
Activities and experiences: Outdoors                           40
Outdoor hideaways                                             42
Frozen fun                                                    44
Buckets of fun                                                46
Spider mania                                                  48
Up and over                                                   50
Roll-a-ball                                                   52
One of our dinosaurs is missing                               54
Lion hunt!                                                    56
Dig and delve                                                 58
Potions and spells                                            60
Speckled frogs                                                62
Beautiful beanstalks                                          64
Parachute fun                                                 66
Further reading and resources                                 68

# Introduction

Communication and Language is one of the three prime areas of learning in the EYFS. It is an area that has historically been identified as key in identifying whether children have reached 'a good level of development', i.e. children should be achieving an 'expected' level in all aspects of Communication and Language, including Speaking ('Talk'). Practitioners need to track children's progress towards the Early Learning Goals (ELGs), and Speaking and Listening, including social communication (which is now embedded within Personal, Social and Emotional Development in the EYFS) needs to be top of the agenda. Talk is the precursor to both reading and writing. Put simply, if children have nothing to say, they will more than likely have nothing to write about.

Dealing with children who are considered to be 'below expectation' in Communication and Language, and in particular in their talk, can be difficult. There is a tendency in many early years settings to identify non-verbal children as having special additional needs and so they are often provided with 'different' activities. This goes against what is actually needed which is excellent practice for all children in promoting high quality talk. Practitioners need to show sensitivity to individual children's existing skills and level of development and then introduce appropriate experiences to support them within a communication friendly learning environment. The activities in this book will extend the communication skills of all children, including those with English as an additional language (EAL) and those at risk of language delay.

The best way for children to increase their receptive vocabulary (the words they understand) and their expressive vocabulary (the words they use) is to be surrounded by adults who talk and listen to them. The most successful way to engage children in verbal communication is by observing them tuning into their passions and interests and then using these to trigger their curiosity as a springboard for learning.

This book is full of tried and tested ideas, activities and adult-led experiences that will support children's communication and language development and in particular, their talk. The majority of activities use everyday objects and require little preparation. There are also suggestions for how to create enabling environments where children have opportunities to lead their own learning and to communicate effectively about things that interest, excite and motivate them.

The Characteristics of Effective Learning underpin children's development and are essential to communication and learning. The relevant characteristics for each activity are clearly highlighted in the book.

# The role of the adult

The role of the adult in supporting children's communication and language development can be complex. Practitioners need to know when to stand back and observe children, when to model vocabulary, and when to make comments or ask leading questions to challenge children's thinking. On occasion, practitioners will:

▶ Provide quiet spaces, both indoors and outdoors, where children can talk away from the general hubbub of the setting, e.g. dens and cosy corners.

▶ Support children's understanding of vocabulary through gestures and actions, paraphrasing where appropriate.

▶ Model active listening to children, providing an interested audience for them to communicate their thoughts, ideas and feelings.

▶ Introduce and model new vocabulary, giving children opportunities to try out new words and play with language.

▶ Listen to children, valuing their attempts to communicate and modelling the next level of language.

▶ Challenge children to explain what they are doing and why, by making comments such as 'I'm not sure I understand what you do next. Can you tell me?'

▶ Engage children in real life experiences such as shopping, gardening and cooking, and support role-play about these familiar experiences, e.g. making 'cups of tea' together and 'putting the baby to bed'.

▶ Value children's invented words to label or describe things or people.

▶ Tell traditional stories which include literary language that children may not yet be familiar with and provide resources such as small world characters, puppets and objects, so that children can retell stories and invent their own.

▶ Share picture books, engaging in dialogic book talk and allowing children to take the lead in retelling stories.

▶ Make collections of interesting objects that will stimulate and interest children.

▶ Involve children in putting together interactive displays about books, stories or objects that interest them.

# Key principles

When we are considering the role of the adult in supporting children's talk, it is important to remember the key principles that underpin talk and support young children's language development (*Every Child a Talker: Guidance for Early Language Lead Practitioners*, DCSF 2008).

1. **Responding sensitively to children's attempts to communicate**

   Whether with a tiny baby who communicates through smiling, cooing and crying, or an older child who uses talk and gestures, the golden rule is to notice what the child is paying attention to or trying to explain, and develop talk around that. The goal is to communicate and talk with the child as partners who respond to each other.

2. **Observing and commenting on the child's current interest**

   A child's language and thinking will develop through interactions with others, and this arises naturally from a shared activity that provides something of interest to talk about, and gives a clear context for words and meanings.

3. **Talking to children in language they are likely to understand**

   Children's language develops when adults support just one step beyond their current language development. Adults can use a range of techniques to build vocabulary, encourage longer utterances, and support use of more complex sentence constructions.

   ▶ **Expansions** – value what the child says by repeating it, and add a little more (e.g. child says, 'Dolly breakfast'; adult says, 'Yes, dolly is eating breakfast.')

   ▶ **Recasts** – provide a language model by changing what the child has said, without changing the meaning (e.g. child says, 'She goed to her grandma's house'; adult says, 'Yes, she went there, didn't she?') Recasts can model correct grammar, sounds of words, or vocabulary (e.g. child says, 'Want cup' while looking at a glass; adult says, 'You want the glass.')

   ▶ **Open-ended questions** – use questions well to encourage children to respond more fully, and to keep the conversation going. Avoid asking too many questions.

4. **Taking time**

   Young language learners need time to gather their thoughts to respond to a question and put it into words. Give children enough time, without jumping in to repeat the question or provide the answer or another comment.

---

**Remember:** try to have a conversation with every child every day. Never underestimate the importance of **phatics** – words and sounds whose purpose is to encourage social communication, e.g. 'mmm', 'uh huh', 'oooh'.

# How to use this book

The book is divided into two sections – the first section focuses on experiences that are based mainly indoors, and the second focuses mainly on outdoor experiences, but some activities are interchangeable. Many of the outdoors experiences will be noisier, messier and should be carried out on a larger scale or using the natural or built environment.

There are suggestions of what children could be learning during each activity, but please remember that learning is not limited to the skills listed. Children, by their very nature, are unpredictable, and so the key to all planning is to be flexible and to think carefully about their specific needs and interests.

Each activity identifies elements of both Enabling Environments and Positive Relationships, including specific vocabulary that can be introduced and modelled, alongside open-ended questions and enabling comments. Each activity includes the following sections:

- ▶ Focus
- ▶ What you could provide
- ▶ What you could do
- ▶ What you could say
- ▶ Another great idea.

## Focus

This section identifies which main aspect of talk the experience focuses on; however, it is important to remember that children may naturally take the learning in another direction, and that this is also fine. For instance, as the practitioner you may have identified that children need support with developing descriptive and comparative vocabulary, and so have introduced a colourful sack filled with soft toys wearing patterned clothes. One child, however, may be excited by rhythmic language and choose to play with words such as 'dotty, spotty, potty, totty...' It is essential that children have access to open-ended resources and that practitioners allow children to lead play and conversation, identifying that this is an example of children's own language learning. The 'Focus' section also describes which Characteristics of Effective Learning the experience supports.

## What you could provide

This section supports Enabling Environments and lists possible resources for each activity. These are only suggestions – you may have your own ideas, or access to different resources. Most of the items listed are readily available in early years settings, and are free or can be sourced cheaply. When you are making collections of items, remember to ask colleagues, families and the wider community if they have any they are willing to donate. Remember, when children are identifying and following their own learning, they will often want to use resources you haven't identified, so make sure they have access to well-organised materials that are clearly labelled with words and photographs.

## What you could do

This section supports Positive Relationships and offers practical ideas of what practitioners can do to support children's developing communication skills. Sometimes this includes modelling the use of specific vocabulary, but on many occasions it will mean offering an audience for children's talk, a 'listening ear' that encourages their attempts to communicate. At other times, the practitioner's role in the activity is about observing and listening patiently, noting what children are doing and saying. If appropriate, adults can join in with children's play, helping them to identify issues that may arise. However, practitioners should avoid taking over or monopolising children's play, or offering 'instant solutions' to problems. In essence, many of the experiences are either about a) interacting and conversing with children, or b) providing time, space and resources in order to observe independent learning and plan follow-up experiences where necessary.

## What you could say

This section includes specific vocabulary to be used, comments that could be made, and open-ended questions that could be asked. You should include these in your planning. It may be helpful to list key questions, comments and specific vocabulary and display these indoors and outdoors, as prompts for both you and the children.

Talk underpins all areas of learning and development; if children do not discuss what they are doing and why they are doing it, it will be very difficult for them to move on in their thinking. Children need opportunities to answer questions, but they also need opportunities to ask them. Practitioners need to provide the scaffolding for children to develop and ask their own questions.

## Another great idea

Many follow-up and extension experiences will evolve from practitioners' observations of children when they are learning. What engages the children? What enthuses them? What are their current passions? This section includes examples of further ideas that will stimulate children and provide opportunities to consolidate their learning.

## Essential resources

Children can, of course, talk about anything across all areas of provision both indoors and outdoors, but access to the following resources will provide them with stimuli for talk:

▶ High-quality picture books, including contemporary stories, traditional tales and books that do not contain words

▶ Traditional and contemporary rhymes and songs

▶ Sound-making resources, e.g. percussion instruments and homemade resources

▶ Electronic recording devices such as sound buttons and talking books, for children to record their own talk

▶ Story props, soft toys and puppets

▶ Dressing up clothes and themed or 'toy' objects to stimulate role play

▶ Small world play collections to stimulate imaginative play

▶ Plants, flowers and vegetables to plant, grow, harvest and cook

▶ Natural objects to explore – fir cones, pebbles, leaves, shells, mud, sand, gravel and more

▶ Living creatures that they can learn about and care for (long term, or on a temporary basis), e.g. hatching chicks or watching caterpillars change into butterflies

▶ Collections of interesting objects, e.g. locks and keys; clocks; shiny objects; treasure; old things; jewellery; toy animals; things that move; noisy things.

# Building vocabulary through dialogic book-sharing

How we read with children is just as important as how often we do it. Often, when sharing a book with one child, an adult will simply read while the child listens. In dialogic reading, children and adults engage in a conversation about the book. The adult becomes an interested listener, a questioner and an audience, meaning that the child becomes the teller of the story.

Dialogic book sharing gives children opportunities to talk about the text and the pictures, allowing them to spend more time on favourite pages and to make connections with their own lives. What's more, adult and child develop a shared understanding of the book.

# Further reading

It is really important that children have access to a wide range of high-quality picture books. These should be available in the book area, and should also have a high profile in all learning zones, both indoors and outdoors. Practitioners should plan to share these stories with individual children and groups, and use them as starting points for sustained interactions. We need to find 'ways into talk' for all children, and books and stories, both contemporary and traditional, can often be the key. CLPE publishes free 'Core Book Lists' online, with information about each text (www.clpe.org.uk). Here are some suggestions of books that promote dialogical book talk.

▶ *Alan's Big, Scary Teeth* by Jarvis (Candlewick Press, 2016)

▶ *Billy's Bucket* by Kes Gray (Red Fox, 2004)

▶ *Biscuit Bear* by Mini Grey (Red Fox, 2005)

▶ *Dear Zoo* by Rod Campbell (Macmillan, 2010)

▶ *Dinosaur Roar!* by Paul and Henrietta Stickland (Corgi, 2014)

▶ *Hoot and Peep* by Lita Judge (Dial Books, 2016)

▶ *I Want My Hat Back* by Jon Klassen (Walker, 2012)

▶ *Jasper's Beanstalk* by Nick Butterworth and Mick Inkpen (Hodder, 2014)

▶ *Lost and Found* by Oliver Jeffers (HarperCollins, 2015)

▶ *Meerkat Mail* by Emily Gravett (Two Hoots, 2015)

▶ *Mr Gumpy's Outing* by John Burningham (Red Fox, 2001)

▶ *On the Way Home* by Jill Murphy (Macmillan, 2007)

▶ *Penguin* by Polly Dunbar (Walker, 2007)

▶ *The Paper Dolls* by Julia Donaldson (Macmillan, 2013)

▶ *We're Going on a Lion Hunt* by David Axtell (Macmillan, 2000)

▶ *Whatever Next!* by Jill Murphy (Macmillan, 2007)

▶ *Where's Spot?* by Eric Hill (Penguin Random House, 2009)

## Traditional and contemporary rhymes

A parental survey revealed that many parents claimed that nursery rhymes were simply too old-fashioned to interest their children (Book Start, 2009). Only just over a third of parents surveyed regularly used nursery rhymes with their children, while almost a quarter admitted that they have never sung a nursery rhyme with their child.

As a result, many children will enter nursery unfamiliar with rhymes, in any language. But we know that rhythm and rhyme and word play are key aspects of early talk, and that children's early knowledge of rhymes promotes later reading development. Studies have demonstrated that the better children are at detecting rhymes, the quicker and more successful they will be at learning to read. (Bradley, 1988, McClean, Bradley & Bryant, Goswami, U. And Bryant, P, 1990.)

# All about me

This indoor experience offers opportunities for children to reflect on and talk about the things that matter to them.

## Focus:

Talk about personal items, family and making links.

## What you could provide:

▶ An empty shoe box per child, already decorated
▶ A set of instructions to go with the box

# What you could do:

▶ Send each child home with a shoe box that they have decorated, and a set of instructions to parents explaining what they and their child should do. With their child, the family should select no more than five special articles to go in the box, such as a special family photo, a favourite toy, a bedtime book, a birthday card, a toy from when they were a baby, or any other significant item that fascinates the child. Be clear that the box should not include food, drink or living items!

▶ Once the child brings the box back to the setting, find time for them to share their box with you, in a group that suits them best. A very shy child may prefer to share their box one-on-one with their key person or with a special friend in a quiet area. A more confident child may be happy to share in a larger group.

▶ For quieter children, be sure to find out key words from their families, e.g. family, pet or toy names, which you can use as verbal prompts.

▶ Help the child to take a photo of the contents of the box, then print this out and add speech bubbles, recording and celebrating the child's talk.

## What you could say:

▶ Invite the child to share the contents of the box, one item at a time. Where appropriate, make comments about the contents, e.g. 'Wow, that's a very sparkly tiara!'.

▶ Build on the child's comments to introduce more vocabulary, e.g. if the child says 'my cat', you could say 'Oh yes, your very fluffy cat'.

▶ Use enabling statements to promote talk, e.g. 'I had a fluffy cat called Ginger'.

▶ Support the child's interactions with other children about their box.

# Another great idea:

▶ Create an 'All About Me' book with the children.

▶ Once the child has brought the box back to the setting, support them in taking a photo of its contents, then stick this photo in the book. Cut out coloured paper speech bubbles and stick them around the image, then fill the speech bubbles with comments from the child about the contents of the box.

▶ Revisit the book at regular intervals and record the children's comments showing developments in their use of talk and increasing vocabulary.

# Spot the Dog

This activity uses Eric Hill's classic picture book as the stimulus for a self-made book about positional language.

## Focus:

Using positional language and maintaining focus for a period of time.

## What you could provide:

▶ Strip of thin card, folded in a concertina to make a large 'zig-zag' book

▶ Photographs of the children

▶ Catalogue pictures of household items – e.g. a rug, wardrobe, table, chair, sofa, bed, curtains – fixed to card to make 'flaps'

▶ Glue stick and markers

▶ *Where's Spot?* by Eric Hill

# What you could do:

▶ Talk to a small group of children about *Where's Spot?* and lift the flaps in the book together.

▶ Choose one child to star in your own version of the book, using the cardboard book you have previously created, and attach an image of the child on the cover.

▶ Complete one page at a time with the children. Fix an image of a different child on each page and cover this photo with a flap. Underneath the picture write an appropriate comment, e.g. 'Where's Sami – is she behind the sofa?', and under the flap write down the name of the corresponding child, e.g. 'No, it's not Sami, it's Yusuf'.

▶ Repeat this structure on each page.

▶ On the final page, place a photo of the starring child under the flap. When the children lift the flap the text should say something like 'Yes, she is! Hello, Sami.'

▶ When the book is complete, support children to retell the story about their friends.

## What you could say:

▶ Remind the children of the text in the original book: 'Where's Spot? Is he under the mat?', and the response 'No, it's Hissing Snake'.

▶ Support the children as they name the objects and use positional language, e.g. 'under, behind, inside, next to...'

▶ Help children to retell the story and remember the names of the other children, e.g. 'That's right, that is Sami – and who is this? Yes, it looks like Freya'.

## Another great idea:

▶ Support children as they make their own zig-zag books about things that interest them, using pictures from magazines, catalogues and photos.

▶ Leave zig-zag books in the mark-making area to encourage independent book making.

# No hiding place

**Young children love to hide in small places, and quiet, cosy spots are great places to talk.**

## Focus:

One-to-one interactions and concentrating for a sustained period of time.

## What you could provide:

▶ A table

▶ Interesting lengths of fabric, cushions, cushions covers, a fluffy rug and other 'cosy' home furnishings

▶ A selection of soft toys and favourite books

# What you could do:

▶ Observe where the children go for 'quiet' conversations, away from adults, and position a table accordingly.

▶ Cover two sides and the back of the table by draping fabric over it, and fix this securely.

▶ Set up a cosy corner under the table, using the rug or small duvet as a base and adding cushions, bean bags etc.

▶ Position yourself so that children can access the area without interruptions, but you can still hear conversations taking place.

▶ Note the children who access the area independently and those who use the space to have chats with friends.

## What you could say:

▶ The adult role for this experience is simply to look, listen and note what children are doing and what they are saying.

▶ Support children as they self regulate and only intervene if essential, e.g. 'Wow, this is a cosy, quiet space – I can see you are talking very quietly here', if the play becomes too boisterous.

## Another great idea:

▶ Create a selection of themed den-making materials for children to choose from: a black and white den with black and white fabrics, zebra print cushions, black and white books; a rainbow den with multi-coloured fabric and cushions and books about rainbows and colours; a sparkly, shiny den with textured fabrics, tinsel and metallic objects.

▶ Create a 'cosy space' where adults and children can interact. Drape fabric from the ceiling and add bean bags or cushions for children to relax on. This creates an environment where children know they can settle down, relax and talk together. Spend some time sitting in the area, talking with children individually or in small groups.

# Little me

**Many children love using characters to support their own storytelling. In this activity they can become the stars of their own stories.**

## Focus:

Using storytelling techniques to explore familiar vocabulary when talking about the self, family and friends.

## What you could provide:

▶ Laminated photographs of each child (these should be about 8cm in height), fixed to small blocks to stand upright

▶ Assorted small world play resources

## What you could do:

▶ Create a small world play scenario around a recent experience that children will remember, e.g. if the children have visited a farm recently, set up a farm scene – add animal figures and any other relevant props.

▶ Place the 'Little Me' characters into the scene and introduce these to the children.

▶ Encourage children to explore the scenario and talk about the characters and resources. Observe what they do and note the language they use.

▶ Prompt children to tell stories about their own and their friends' experiences.

▶ Write down the children's stories and then read them together.

## What you could say:

▶ Make comments about the positioning of the 'Little Me' characters, e.g. 'It looks as though you have fallen over. I remember when you fell over at the farm. Do you remember what happened?'.

▶ Introduce and model vocabulary, e.g. cow and calf; horse and foal; pig and piglet; sheep and lamb; duck and duckling.

▶ Extend children's talk, e.g. if the child says 'Got my boots on', you could say 'Yes, you have got your big muddy boots on'.

▶ Repeat correct words back to children (but don't expect children to copy), e.g. if the child says 'I runned all the way', say 'Wow – you ran all the way?'.

## Another great idea:

▶ Supplement specific small world play collections with special themed 'Little Me' characters, e.g. make emergency services 'Little Me' characters by taking photographs of the children dressed up as fire fighters, doctors, police officers and paramedics.

▶ Consider adding laminated photographs of the local environment – shops, school, places of worship, tower blocks, bus stops etc.

# Read all about it!

Books are a great source of new vocabulary for children – especially those that ignite emotions, such as happiness, sadness or even disgust!

## Focus:

Talk exploring imagination, including slightly scary things, and linking experiences.

## What you could provide:

▶ A copy of *Biscuit Bear* by Mini Grey

## What you could do:

▶ Familiarise yourself with the book *Biscuit Bear*, thinking about possible tangents for discussion.

▶ Read the book with one or two children in a comfy, quiet space.

▶ Make sure the child or children are familiar with the story – ideally, this should be a book that they have chosen to revisit (you can substitute *Biscuit Bear* for a different book if children prefer).

▶ Choose one child to 'tell' the story in their own words. It is important to follow their lead, allowing them to pause and focus on favourite parts of the tale – encourage them to discuss this and engage them in conversation.

▶ Act as an interested audience to the child telling the story, modelling active listening to other children in the group.

## What you could say:

▶ Ask children if they can explain what is happening on each page, encouraging sustained conversation. Avoid asking too many questions.

▶ Build on the child's comments by asking clarifying questions, e.g. if the child says 'scary dog', prompt them to explain why they think the dog is scary.

▶ Use enabling statements, e.g. 'I had a big, fluffy dog once, his name was Charlie'.

▶ Support interactions between the child reading, and the child listening.

▶ Emphasise new or more difficult vocabulary to increase comprehension, e.g. 'I wonder what that acrobat will do next?'

## Another great idea:

▶ *Biscuit Bear* is a great stimulus for a cooking activity; make simple biscuit dough, shape it into bears and bake.

▶ Support children as they decorate biscuit bears with icing, hundreds and thousands, glace cherries and candied peel.

▶ Remember to talk about what you are doing and why throughout the activity.

# Any old iron?

This experience gives children the opportunity to explore metal objects and other shiny materials.

## Focus:

Developing descriptive and comparative vocabulary and learning to hypothesise.

## What you could provide:

▶ A metal chest (the larger, the better) filled with some familiar and some unfamiliar metal objects and other shiny materials, e.g. coins, metallic clothing etc.

▶ Shiny or sparkly fabric to cover the chest

# What you could do:

- ▶ Show the covered chest to the children. Encourage them to guess what could be under the fabric.

- ▶ Uncover the chest together and discuss what could be inside it.

- ▶ Taking it in turns, ask children to choose one object from the chest and talk about it. What do they think it is? Where has it come from?

- ▶ Allow the children time to explore the items in the chest, e.g. by dressing up in a shiny cape, or balancing coins on a metal tray.

- ▶ Observe the children and note the language they use. Are they concentrating on describing the objects? Are they hypothesising what things are, or using their imaginations?

## What you could say:

- ▶ Support children's conversations, encouraging them to formulate questions as well as answers.

- ▶ Prompt the children's desire to find out more about the items, e.g. 'I wonder if there is another key for that padlock?'

- ▶ Use enabling statements, e.g. 'I had a clock like that a long time ago, I had to wind it up every day'.

- ▶ Model specific descriptive vocabulary, e.g. if children are using magnets, explain the terms 'magnetic' and 'non-magnetic' or introduce the names of different metals such as iron, silver, gold, tin and brass.

- ▶ Promote links with children's experiences at home, e.g. 'Wow – so your great grandad has a trunk filled with uniforms'.

## Another great idea:

- ▶ Create an interactive display using the objects.

- ▶ Display information about metals and collectables, and add magnets, magnifiers and lots of coins for children to explore.

- ▶ You can add to this by putting up images of the children exploring the objects and comments about what they observed.

# Kim's Game

**This game uses familiar objects to introduce children to nouns and extend their descriptive and comparative vocabulary in a fun way.**

## Focus:

Developing children's vocabulary of naming and describing objects (nouns and verbs) and encouraging attention to detail.

## What you could provide:

▶ A tray with a collection of interesting objects – for younger children you will only need a small number of objects (three or four), for older children or those with a wider vocabulary you will need a larger number (up to 12)

▶ A piece of fabric, large enough to cover all the objects

# What you could do:

▶ Place the collection in front of the children. Give them time to explore and talk about the objects.

▶ Once the children are familiar with the items, name them together. Agree on the vocabulary you will use for items with more than one possible name, e.g. is it a mug or a cup, a teddy or a bear?

▶ Hide the objects under the fabric. Remove one object without the children seeing.

▶ Uncover the tray and see if children can identify the missing object. If nobody knows, describe the object until someone guesses correctly.

▶ Repeat this until children are familiar with the game, and then support them as they take the lead, removing an object and asking the other children what is missing.

## What you could say:

▶ Ask the child to talk about the contents of the tray, one item at a time. Make comments when appropriate, e.g. 'That's a very soft powder puff'.

▶ Build on the children's comments, e.g. if the child says 'Car gone', you could say 'Yes, the racing car has gone'.

▶ Use enabling statements, e.g. 'I think I like the gold star best'.

▶ Support children's interactions with one another.

## Another great idea:

▶ Set up a permanent interactive display, providing a collection of interesting objects and baskets, trays, bowls, boxes and bags for children to put them in. Choose objects based on children's current interests. You could do this thematically or randomly. Write down children's comments and add these to the display.

▶ Regularly replace the objects in the collection, to maintain interest and prevent boredom.

# Tiny treasures

**This activity allows children to get into the role of a pirate and have fun exploring shiny treasure!**

## Focus:

Developing children's descriptive vocabulary; the importance of taking turns in communication.

## What you could provide:

▶ A treasure chest filled with necklaces, watches, bangles, badges, coins, jewels, chunky plastic rings and other small shiny objects

▶ A selection of magnifying glasses, tweezers and small jewellery boxes

▶ Pirate hats and eye patches

## What you could do:

▶ Put the objects in the treasure chest and place it on the floor in a quiet area.

▶ Observe the children as they play with the objects. Which children engage in role play?

▶ If invited, join in as a co-player, following the children's play themes.

▶ Note the names of children who: engage in solitary play, initiate conversations with others, and listen carefully and respond.

## What you could say:

▶ Support the child's interactions with others – model the use of naming words and descriptive vocabulary, e.g. 'You are right, that ring is much bigger than that one' or 'I think that's called a pocket watch – I wonder why?'

▶ Model active listening to children when they are talking and explain this is what you are doing, e.g. 'I am listening to you'.

▶ Encourage shared sustained conversations with children, e.g. 'So your mum has a necklace like that one, does she?'.

▶ Get into the role by using language associated with pirates, e.g. 'Shiver me timbers!'

▶ Extend children's talk, e.g. 'Yes, that is a super ring – it's a very sparkly, glittery ring.'

## Another great idea:

▶ Develop a pirate role-play area outdoors. Turn the climbing frame into a ship or create one out of large cardboard packing boxes.

▶ Embellish the area with treasure chests, flags, pirate paraphernalia and costumes.

▶ Bury 'treasure' in the sandpit or elsewhere in the outdoor area and provide children with treasure maps, shovels, sieves, spades and buckets.

▶ Set up a small table activity with dry sand, tea strainers, sequins and small jewels for children to explore.

# Feeling good

This activity builds on children's natural curiosity by encouraging them to put things into, and take them out of, containers.

## Focus:

Develop children's use of descriptive vocabulary; encouraging them to ask and answer questions.

## What you could provide:

*I will need*

▶ A 'Feely Box' – make this from an empty cardboard box with a lid

▶ A collection of objects of differing shapes, sizes and textures, e.g. a shell, a teddy, a wooden car, a clock, a glove, a ball, an orange, a sponge and a leather purse

## What you could do:

▶ Decorate the box so that it looks interesting. Cut a hole in the lid that is large enough for you to fit your hand inside.

▶ Place all the objects in the box – make sure each can be removed through the hole, without removing the lid.

▶ Choose a volunteer, preferably a child who has a wider vocabulary, to feel inside the box and choose one object without removing it from the box. This will provide a model for other children.

## What you could say:

▶ Ask the child to describe the object they can feel, prompting where necessary, e.g. 'Is it soft, or hard?', 'Do you think it is something you could eat?'.

▶ Build on the child's comments, e.g. if the child says 'cold and hard', prompt them further: 'If it is cold and hard, I wonder if it is like a stone?' or 'Oh, it's not like a stone, but it is cold and hard... I wonder if it is like a car?'

▶ Help the other children to ask questions, e.g. 'If you want to know if it is big, what could you ask?'. Help them to ask broad questions instead of asking in lists ('Is it a ball?', 'Is it a car?', 'Is it a teddy?').

▶ If appropriate, model descriptive vocabulary by choosing an object, e.g. 'It is something to eat', 'It is the same shape as a ball', 'It's quite soft', 'It is rough, not smooth', 'It's not an apple, but it is a fruit', and finally, 'That's right, it's an orange'.

▶ When a child guesses correctly, look at the object together and recap any the descriptive vocabulary that was used.

## Another great idea:

▶ Fill two bags with identical objects.

▶ Support as they take turns to describe an object that they can feel in pairs.

29

# A box of delights

**Use exciting boxes and intriguing props to support young children's exploration of narrative.**

## Focus:

Introducing story telling techniques, allowing children to show particular interests.

## What you could provide:

I will need

▶ A shoe box – this will become your 'story box'

▶ Scissors and paper in assorted colours and textures

▶ A small collection of key props, characters and artifacts to support fantasy stories, e.g. giants, monsters, fairies, unicorns, broomstick, magic wand, treasure box, gold coins etc.

## What you could do:

▶ Cut down two corners of the shoe box – this will form the 'stage'.

▶ Decorate the shoe box to reflect the story you will create inside. Choose a theme that the children are interested in and may have explored already, e.g. for a story about magic, cover the box with shiny paper and silver stars.

▶ Place relevant props in the box and replace the lid.

▶ Show the box to a small group of children in a comfy, quiet space.

▶ Allow children time to tell their own stories, using the props.

▶ Write down the children's stories in a 'special' book.

## What you could say:

▶ Model the use of the specific vocabulary, so if a child is waving a wand around, you could say 'abracadabra', or 'Wow, that sounds like a great spell'.

▶ If the children begin to struggle, support them by using prompts, e.g. 'So the fairy made the little girl fall asleep. I wonder what happened next?'

▶ Expand the children's comments, e.g. if a child says 'big giant', add more descriptive vocabulary – for instance, 'Wow! A huge, enormous giant'.

▶ Encourage children to reflect on any new vocabulary, e.g. 'I wonder what that unicorn will do next?'

## Another great idea:

▶ Make some more story boxes with the children, building on their ideas and interests.

▶ Create boxes based on favourite books.

▶ Ensure children have access to the boxes to support independent story-telling.

# Tell me a story

**Use magnetic story props to support children's retelling of their favourite tales.**

## Focus:

Involving children in retelling stories, using literary language and encouraging concentration.

## What you could provide:

▶ A copy of the book *Whatever Next?* by Jill Murphy

▶ A large magnetic storyboard, magnetic wedge, or large tin tray

▶ Drawings of key characters and objects – mummy bear, baby bear, the owl, a box, wellington boots, a colander, the moon, a bath, and a bed

*I will need*

# What you could do:

▶ Laminate the drawings and stick a strip of magnetic tape on the reverse. Take copies of drawings and store these safely in case any get lost.

▶ Introduce the magnetic props to the children and talk about the characters and objects – what could Baby Bear use the colander and the box for?

▶ If the children are unfamiliar with magnetic props, model how to use them.

▶ Record the children's versions of the story and their new stories.

## What you could say:

▶ Encourage the children's own conversations about the story, modelling careful listening.

▶ Consolidate children's retelling of the story, e.g. 'That's right, Baby Bear wants a space helmet'.

▶ Use enabling statements, e.g. 'If I was having a picnic, I would like cheese sandwiches and apple slices'.

▶ Help the children to follow the sequence of a story: 'That was a great beginning to your story – what happens next?' or 'Is that the end of your story?'.

# Another great idea:

▶ Provide a child size collection of props from the story – a cardboard box big enough to get into, a real colander, wellington boots, a soft toy owl, and a cardboard moon.

▶ Encourage children to make up their own journeys into space.

▶ If invited, join in with children's role play.

# We're all going on a summer holiday

**Many children are interested in traveling and talking about their holidays, so use this opportunity to talk about the future.**

## Focus:

Using future tenses and acting out experiences in role play.

## What you could provide:

▶ Small or child-sized suitcases

▶ A laundry basket filled with holiday clothes, including an assortment of shoes, beachwear and clothes for cold weather

▶ Beach equipment, including flippers, goggles, beach balls, rubber ring, buckets, spades, arm bands and sun hats

## What you could do:

▶ Help the children to pack items for their holiday in a case – do they need clothes for hot weather and the beach, or clothes for cold weather or skiing?

▶ Notice which children choose items for a specific purpose and which children simply fill the case to the brim with the nearest objects to hand.

## What you could say:

▶ Talk to children about holidays they have been on in the past. How did they get there (car, train, plane)? Was it hot or cold? Did they go to a beach?

▶ Model the use of future tenses, e.g. 'I am holidaying in England, so I will drive my car', 'I will stay in a caravan and go to the beach'.

▶ Support children in talking about their planned holidays, e.g. if a child says 'I go beach', repeat back 'How lovely – you will go to the beach! I will go to the beach too'.

▶ Ask questions that encourage children to expand, e.g. 'How did the suitcase break? What did you do then?'

## Another great idea:

▶ Create a role-play scenario based on what children tell you about their holidays, e.g. transform the outdoor sand pit into a beach and add buckets and spades, wind breakers, towels etc. Add an ice cream stall and a paddling pool 'sea'. Support children's role-play in the area.

# Gruffalo magic

In this activity children have the opportunity to retell a favourite tale and make up some of their own stories, too.

## Focus:

Retelling and creating stories, recognising different patterns and structures.

## What you could provide:

▶ A copy of *The Gruffalo* by Julia Donaldson

▶ A collection of soft toys or wooden or plastic animals to represent characters in the book, e.g. the Gruffalo, a mouse, a fox, an owl and a snake

# What you could do:

▶ Introduce the characters to children, allowing them time to explore them. Observe and listen to them as they do this.

▶ Some children will link the resources to the familiar story straight away but others might need some prompting, so be on hand to provide support.

▶ Note down the names of children who retell the whole story or parts of it, those who act out the characters and those who create a new story.

## What you could say:

▶ Support children to use rhythmic text from the book, e.g. 'He has terrible tusks, and terrible claws, and terrible teeth in his terrible jaws.'

▶ With younger children or those with less expressive vocabulary, point out characteristics of the Gruffalo and talk about them, e.g. 'Look – he has got long, pointy claws'.

▶ If they get stuck when telling the story, recite a little of it yourself so children can join in.

▶ Support less confident children by using gestures as well as props, e.g. by growling and showing your teeth or 'claws'.

▶ If children begin to develop the story by adding new characters or inventing a new part of story, encourage them with open-ended questions, e.g. 'I wonder what happened then?'

## Another great idea:

▶ Get children on their feet and ask them if they can move like an owl, a snake, a mouse, a fox or the Gruffalo.

▶ Set up a walking route in the outdoor area with the children. Fix the characters onto boxes or plastic cones at different points on the route for children to discover.

▶ As you move through the route, retell the story with the children.

# What's next?

Children with limited receptive vocabulary can find it difficult to understand daily routines, which may heighten their anxiety levels. This activity will help alleviate these negative emotions.

## Focus:

Developing an understanding of the sequence of different events.

## What you could provide:

▶ A display summarising the key events that happen in a normal day

# What you could do:

▶ Identify key elements of a day in your setting – what do children do during their time with you? E.g. they arrive, they play indoors, they have a snack, they play outdoors, they tidy up, they have a story, songs and rhymes and then they go home. Routines vary in each setting so it is important to include key aspects, for example lunchtime or sleep time.

▶ Take photographs of each part of the day – keep these clear and simple.

▶ Show the photographs to children in small groups and talk about what is happening and why. Ask children to help you write a few words describing each of them, and then add these to the display.

▶ Refer to the display throughout the day, or to individual children when they need reminding what happens next.

## What you could say:

▶ Show children you value the comments they make about the photographs by repeating and expanding upon them, e.g. 'Tidy time! That's right, it's tidy up time, so now we will put the toys away.'

▶ Encourage children to think and use their initiative, e.g. 'I wonder what happens when we have finished playing outside?'

▶ Model language explaining the sequence of events, e.g. 'After we arrive, we play indoors and then we choose to play indoors or outdoors', and 'After we tidy up, we read a story together and then we sing songs before we go home'.

## Another great idea:

▶ Make photographic sequences of specific events, e.g. of the lunch routine – washing and drying hands before eating, eating our lunch, washing our hands again and then putting lunch boxes away.

▶ Make two sets of photographs, then display one in the appropriate area and use the other to support discussions about the routines with children.

# Trip trap, trip trap: Three Billy Goats Gruff

Give the children plenty of time and space to act out a favourite tale outdoors.

## Focus:

Introducing children to different vocabulary for size and comparison; acting out experiences with other people.

## What you could provide:

I will need

▶ A 'bridge' – this could be made from large hollow wooden blocks, a plank, or a tree stump

▶ A 'river' – a long strip of blue fabric

# What you could do:

▶ Ensure that the children are familiar the *Three Billy Goats Gruff* story.

▶ Spend some time with the children, finding out more about the Billy Goats Gruff and the troll, e.g. how does the Big Billy Goat Gruff walk and talk? What about the smallest Billy Goat Gruff? How does the troll jump out?

▶ Take turns walking over the 'bridge', trying out different ways of moving.

▶ Support the children as they retell the story, acting in role.

▶ If the children are retelling the story independently, record their version.

## What you could say:

▶ Support children who are struggling to re-tell the story by reminding them of the sequence of events, e.g. 'Where is the troll at the beginning of the story?', or 'Who is the first Billy Goat Gruff to cross the bridge?'.

▶ Prompt children with key pieces of rhythmic text, e.g. 'Up jumped the troll, and he roared, 'Who's that going over my bridge?''

▶ With less confident children, act in role, modeling story book language, e.g. 'Trip trap, trip trap, the Little Billy Goat Gruff went over the bridge to the lush grass on the other side'.

## Another great idea:

▶ Make a *Three Billy Goats Gruff* story box with the children.

▶ Use props when re-telling the story, e.g. soft toy goats (of varying size), a troll, blocks to make a bridge, fake grass, a blue fabric or paper river.

▶ Record children's talk using a sound tin or tablet.

# Outdoor hideaways

**This exciting activity combines being outdoors with finding places to hide – a magical formula for many children.**

## Focus:

Encouraging shared, sustained conversations without distractions.

## What you could provide:

**For the broomsticks:**

▶ Broom handles, buckets, quick-setting cement, tape and clips (adult-only step)

**For the den:**

▶ Camouflage netting, tarpaulin, backpacks, camping equipment, torches, maps

# What you could do:

▶ Before involving the children, make broomstick poles:

▷ Place four broom handles vertically in four builders' buckets.

▷ Pour quick-setting ready mixed cement into the bucket to secure the broom handles.

▷ Fix large, plastic covered hooks to the top of the sticks and attach tape and fabric.

▶ With children, find a suitable location in your outdoor area and introduce them to the den-making materials.

▶ Instruct children to build a den using the materials you have provided. While they are building, talk about why they have chosen certain materials and ways in which the fabric can be fixed to the broomstick poles. Help the children to explore different ways of draping and attaching the fabric to the broomsticks to make their covered hideaway.

▶ Respond to children's suggestions for additions to the den – they may have ideas that include using home corner resources.

▶ If invited, play with children in their dens. Ask questions, e.g. 'what is it like to be an explorer?' or 'what's it like to hide away quietly in a small cave?'

▶ Be flexible and allow children to lead play – you may be planning an exploration, but the children may prefer to have a picnic.

## What you could say:

▶ Get into character, using appropriate language, e.g. 'so where are we going tomorrow? What do we need in our backpacks?'

▶ Encourage children to extend their speech and ideas, e.g. 'so we are going to find the treasure – I wonder where we will travel to?'

▶ Support children to in asking and answering questions.

## Another great idea:

▶ Create a den-making area in your setting, making sure resources are easy for children to access independently. Replace cardboard boxes regularly, as these quickly become damaged, and include waterproof materials such as shower curtains.

# Frozen fun

It is always important to focus on children's current interests – and this means embracing popular culture. If children are fascinated by all things *Frozen*, incorporate this into your planning.

## Focus:

Scientific vocabulary about change and materials; using senses to explore the world around them.

## What you could provide:

▶ Toys or small world models, including a selection of sea life creatures and animals that live in cold climates

▶ Assorted plastic bowls

▶ Food colouring

▶ Sequins and glitter

▶ Natural objects – branches, boulders, seashells etc.

▶ A large builders' tray or 'grow bag' tray

# What you could do:

▶ Pour a small amount of water into each plastic bowl.

▶ Add one or two creatures to each bowl, adding glitter, sequins or food colouring if desired.

▶ Fill bowls to the brim and freeze overnight.

▶ Tip the ice out onto the tray, adding natural objects.

▶ Allow children to explore the new small world play environment (make sure they're wearing gloves).

▶ Encourage children if they begin to make links with home experiences.

## What you could say:

▶ Listen to children's use of vocabulary and model specific vocabulary when appropriate, e.g. 'Yes, it looks like a whale'.

▶ Talk to the children about what they are doing and why, e.g. 'Tia, can you tell me why you moved that big block of ice into the sunshine?'

▶ Encourage the children to hypothesise about what can be discovered in the ice, e.g. 'I can see something in the ice, what do you think it is?', 'I wonder what will happen when all the ice melts?' or 'how do you think we could make more ice?'.

## Another great idea:

▶ Revisit the activity and involve children from the outset by providing a water tray filled with ice and allow children to hide or make ice cubes.

▶ On cold days, explore the outdoors together – is there frost, ice on puddles, icicles or snow?

# Buckets of fun

This experience builds on children's fascination with 'knowing best' and supports storytelling using props.

## Focus:

Introducing children to specific vocabulary; using objects to represent things from their experience.

## What you could provide:

▶ A copy of *Billy's Bucket* by Kes Gray and Garry Parsons (2004)

▶ A paddling pool filled with water

▶ Assorted seaside buckets of different sizes, materials and designs (one for each child)

▶ Under-the-sea props, including lots of natural objects such as sand, pebbles, seaweed and shells

I will need

# What you could do:

▶ Familiarise children with the story – you could substitute *Billy's Bucket* for another similarly themed story if you prefer.

▶ Place the objects in the paddling pool for children to discover and explore in small groups.

▶ Ask each child to select several items from the pool to add to their bucket.

▶ The children must then use the objects inside the bucket to tell their own story.

## What you could say:

▶ While reading the story, encourage children to join in with repeated refrains, e.g. 'You must never, ever, ever borrow my bucket'.

▶ Invite children to share the contents of their buckets, using language taken from the story to do so – 'What can you see when you peer inside your bucket?' 'What does each object do?'

▶ Model the use of specific vocabulary – if the child is talking about 'fish', offer a specific name. You could also talk about different types of sea creatures, both real and fictional.

## Another great idea:

▶ Create an interactive display, using the children's buckets and objects. Include large images of the objects and label these with speech bubbles with children's stories or descriptions of them.

# Spider mania

The activity is popular with children who are interested in minibeasts – and using a traditional rhyme, also works well with children who are anxious about spiders.

## Focus:

Introduce children to traditional rhymes, using gestures and turn-taking.

## What you could provide:

▶ A basket filled with an assorted collection of pretend spiders, e.g. puppets and plastic toys.

▶ Short lengths of plastic drainpipe and plastic tubes

I will need

# What you could do:

▶ Together, learn the traditional nursery rhyme 'Incy Wincy Spider', and repeat until the children are familiar with it. Then introduce the collection of toy spiders.

▶ Support the children as they investigate the collection of spiders. Observe what they do and what they say. Encourage children who link the resources to the rhyme – some may begin to chant.

▶ Encourage open play and investigations with the toy spiders, making sure the lengths of drainpipe and tubing are easily accessible.

▶ If children are anxious about the spiders, or try to frighten others, focus on the caring aspects of looking after small creatures.

## What you could say:

▶ Support children's conversations, encouraging them to formulate questions as well as answers.

▶ If the children make connections with the familiar rhyme, support them as they retell it, or start chanting the rhyme and see who joins in.

▶ Support less confident children by modelling the actions and gestures.

▶ Use enabling statements, e.g. 'I wonder if that spider really will fit in that spout?'

# Another great idea:

▶ Use chalks to draw 'drainpipes' on the floor, with ten spaces on each, a start and an end.

▶ Cover a large dice with the following pictures: rain, sun and one, two, three and four dots. Use a toy spider as a playing piece.

▶ Support the children as they develop 'rules' for the game, e.g. if you roll a two, move the spider two spaces along the pipe. If you roll a 'rain', return to the bottom. What could it mean if the dice lands on 'sunshine'?

# Up and over

We all know children who prefer to be physically active outdoors and rarely speak indoors. This experience gives them a chance to develop positional language while doing something they love.

## Focus:

The use of positional vocabulary and verbs; showing a 'have a go' attitude.

## What you could provide:

I will need

▶ Use whatever freestanding outdoor equipment you have available to create an obstacle course

▶ Add fixed camouflage netting or fabric for children to crawl under and huge boxes for them to get inside or crawl through

▶ Make sure you have things to get under, over, on top of and through

▶ Add numbers or arrows to show the route around the course

## What you could do:

▶ Set up the obstacle course for children to explore.

▶ Make sure children and any other staff assisting you use the same set of safety rules.

▶ Notice which children play alone, those who play in groups and those who talk to each other about what they are doing.

▶ Support children as they make their way around the obstacle course, talking about where they are going next.

### What you could say:

▶ Invite the children to share what they are doing and why.

▶ Build on the child's comments, e.g. If the child says 'up, up', say 'yes, up high'.

▶ Model the use of positional language as the children move around, e.g. 'Sammi is under the blanket' or 'Ben is going through the tunnel'.

▶ Support the child's interactions with other children about the obstacles.

## Another great idea:

▶ Introduce the language of movement. Give children opportunities to move around the outdoor area in whatever way they choose, and take photos.

▶ Laminate the images of the children and the matching vocabulary and display in the outdoor area, e.g. jumping, crawling, climbing, walking, running, skipping, hopping. Model the use of the different vocabulary as the children move around and refer to the images.

# Roll-a-ball

**Younger children often enjoy backwards and forwards ball rolling – this can easily be turned into an outdoor game to develop talk.**

## Focus:

Turn taking and thinking of ideas.

## What you could provide:

▶ A ball – a soft ball or one that lights up will work well

## What you could do:

▶ Before you start, talk about a specific group of things that the children are interested in, such as wild animals, using appropriate vocabulary e.g. the names of the animals.

▶ Sit opposite one child, so that you are in a pair, and roll the ball towards them. As you do so, call out the name of a wild animal. Ask the child to roll the ball back to you, repeating the name. Repeat this several times with the child, calling out the names of different animals.

▶ With older children, or those with a wider or more expressive vocabulary, sit in a circle as a group and let the children take turns to call out an animal name and roll the ball to another child. This child then calls another animal name and rolls the ball to another child, and so on.

## What you could say:

▶ Involve children in the creation of the list you will use, e.g. for wild animals – lion, tiger, giraffe, zebra, antelope, rhinoceros, chimpanzee.

▶ Prompt children who are quiet or withdrawn to add to the list by asking 'I wonder if there are more wild animals we haven't thought of?'

▶ If there are suggestions that do not fit into the category, discuss why, e.g. 'Could a pig be a wild animal? Could it live in the jungle?'

▶ As the children roll the ball, help them to choose an animal name to call, e.g. 'Can you think of a big wild animal?, or 'Can you think of a fierce wild animal?'

▶ Model your thinking as you list the animals by pointing to your head as you speak, e.g. 'Mm, we've had zebra, giraffe, leopard, crocodile, I think I'll say hippopotamus!'

## Another great idea:

▶ Make two different collections of objects, e.g. a collection of wild animals and a collection of cars and trucks.

▶ Mix the collections up in one large basket. Ask children to take turns to take an object and sort it into the correct basket. Use an adjective for each object, e.g. 'fast car', 'tall giraffe', 'enormous elephant', 'shiny car'.

▶ Use this strategy when tidying up – challenge children to put away resources into the correct trays, boxes and baskets.

# One of our dinosaurs is missing

This game is similar to **Hide and Seek**, but enables children to seek out missing objects together.

## Focus:

Following instructions; positional vocabulary; working together.

## What you could provide:

▶ A collection of toy dinosaurs (preferably quite large in size)

# What you could do:

▶ Explore the collection of dinosaurs with children, talking about the size, colours and characteristics of each creature.

▶ Hide the dinosaurs in the outdoor area – make some very easy to find and others a little more challenging.

▶ Support the children as they search for the missing dinosaurs – giving them clues where necessary.

▶ Notice which children follow instructions and directions and those who continue to search randomly.

▶ When all the dinosaurs are found, allow two children to hide the dinosaurs again (limit the search area as necessary).

▶ Help the 'hiders' to give other children instructions and clues as they search.

# What you could say:

▶ Introduce children to specific vocabulary – 'tyrannosaurus rex', 'diplodocus', 'stegosaurus', 'triceratops' and 'pterodactyl'.

▶ Support the children's use of descriptive language, e.g. 'That's right Danni, the dinosaur with the very long tail is still missing'.

▶ Give the children instructions to follow, e.g. 'You need to walk towards the climbing frame', 'Now look upwards'.

▶ Support the children as they give instructions to each other, e.g. 'Where does Cheri need to go now?'.

▶ Model the use of positional vocabulary, e.g. 'Yes Simon, it's underneath the slide' or 'Oh look – it's next to the sand pit!'

# Another great idea:

▶ Design 'missing' posters for the hidden objects with the children. Use photographic images and children's drawings.

▶ Write down children's descriptions of the missing creatures, encouraging the use of descriptive and comparative vocabulary.

▶ Help children to display the posters in the outdoor area.

# Lion hunt!

**Build on the children's interest in a favourite tale and give them time and space to act out the journey outdoors.**

## Focus:

Using rhythmic and positional language; following instructions.

## What you could provide:

▶ A copy of the book *We're Going on a Lion Hunt* by David Axtell

▶ A large outdoor area, with space to set up a trail

## What you could do:

► Set up a trail outdoors that loosely follows the journey in the book – try to include things for children to climb through. Use a sandpit as a desert or swamp, a paddling pool as a lake and arrange plants, logs and lengths of fabric in creative ways.

► Read the book and see if children can join in with some of the repetitive text.

► Next, give children time to explore the trail – observe what they do and say.

► Notice if any children link the trail to the story or use part of the text in their play.

## What you could say:

► Support children's conversations and encourage them to narrate what they are doing, e.g. 'I'm stamping through the long grass.'

► If the children make connections with the book, help them to retell the story, or start chanting parts of the text and see who joins in.

## Another great idea:

► Create more trails with the children. Explore different ways of moving – skipping, hopping, jumping, rolling, running or crawling. Model the use of verbs and support the children as they use the language.

► Play 'Follow the Leader', moving around the outdoor area in different ways. As children gain confidence, let them take the lead and give instructions to others.

# Dig and delve

This physical learning experience gives children the opportunity to make links with home experiences.

## Focus:

Developing knowledge of verbs; working together collaboratively.

## What you could provide:

▶ Assorted wellington boots, position these on a boot stand

▶ Gardening equipment – shovels, spades, forks, buckets, watering cans, wheelbarrows, hoes, sieves, flower pots plastic and silk flowers

▶ Access to water – an outdoor tap, hose or water butt

## What you could do:

▶ Clear an outdoor digging area, and make children aware they can visit it whenever they wish to.

▶ Store the digging tools and wellington boots somewhere where they can be accessed independently.

▶ Ensure children have appropriate clothing for digging and getting muddy – provide waterproof coveralls if necessary.

▶ Talk to the children as they interact with one another while digging and filling and emptying buckets.

## What you could say:

▶ Name the tools with the children, using specific vocabularly. Ask if they know what can they be used for.

▶ Encourage children to talk about home experiences – have they got gardens? Have they experience of digging with family or friends?

▶ Remind children of any events when they would have seen workers digging at your setting, e.g. 'Do you remember when the gardeners planted the new hedges?' or 'I remember when the workers put the new paving stones in front of the gate'.

## Another great idea:

▶ Create a water wall with the children. Make sure there is easy access to a water supply.

▶ Drill holes into funnels, guttering, pipes and plastic bottles, and fix these at angles on a fence or wooden board. Make sure that any water that is poured down the pieces of guttering or tubing flows into a funnel or bottle.

▶ Provide children with mugs, bottles, jugs, bowls and other containers to use in their water play.

▶ Have towels to hand in case of spillages.

▶ Display vocabulary related to and about water near taps or outside water supplies.

# Potions and spells

Mud kitchens are a very popular feature in most early years settings. This 'mud laboratory' offers children the chance to link messy play with fantasy tales.

## Focus:

Using vocabulary that is linked to a role; showing children to use objects to represent different items in their play.

## What you could provide:

▶ Wooden benches at child height

▶ A metal sink

▶ Plastic conical flasks, plastic test tubes, assorted containers, wooden and metal spoons and ladles

▶ Mixing bowls, bottles with lids and 'cauldrons'

▶ Laminated recipes or spells

▶ Natural objects, e.g. pebbles, shells, twigs, gravel, leaves, conkers, pine cones, petals, sand

▶ Appropriate dressing up costumes, e.g. white coats, aprons, cloaks and magicians' hats

# What you could do:

▶ Set up the mud laboratory. It is a good idea to position it near to plants that children can pick – scented leaves including herbs are particularly useful.

▶ Encourage the children to explore the laboratory. Observe the ways in they use the area – who uses it in a scientific way? Who has a go at mixing potions or making spells?

▶ When invited, join in as co-player. Follow children's play themes and take on a role, e.g. a scientist experimenting or a wizard mixing potions and casting spells.

## What you could say:

▶ Prompt children to express their thoughts, e.g. 'Yes, that is a smelly leaf, Kieran... I can't think what it smells like...'

▶ Use language related to specific roles e.g. 'hubble, bubble, toil and trouble', 'whizzity whiz, whizzity woo'.

▶ Respond to children's play themes, e.g. 'Thank you very much for the medicine Sarah, I hope it makes me better'; 'What? You've tricked me? It's poison, oh no!'

▶ Help children to share recipes and instructions, e.g. 'First you mixed the mint leaves and the water. Then you added a cup of gravel and stirred that around. What did you do next?'

# Another great idea:

▶ Make 'petal perfume' with the children. Collect assorted petals – rose petals work particularly well. Provide small bottles, bowls, jugs, lids, labels and a pestle and mortar. Help the children to combine the petals with water to make their own perfume.

# Speckled frogs

Living things excite and motivate children. This experience teaches children about how creatures grow, and lets them observe newborn creatures first-hand.

## Focus:

Specific vocabulary related to and about frogs; recognising the need to care for living things.

## What you could provide:

▶ Frog spawn

▶ Books about frogs and tadpoles

▶ A camera

▶ Magnifying glasses

## What you could do:

▶ Locate frog spawn at a safe and accessible area that you have permission to visit – a friend's garden pond is ideal.

▶ Set up the books and magnifying glasses close to the pond.

▶ Show the frog spawn to a small group of children, explaining what it is and observing their reactions.

▶ Let children carefully examine the frog spawn and remind them of the care they need to take with fragile living things. Write down any comments they make.

▶ Once the spawn has developed into frogs, revisit them with the children and take photographs to create a display.

## What you could say:

▶ Introduce specific language related to growth and change, with reference to frogs in particular, e.g. spawn, tadpole, froglet, frog, life cycle.

▶ Ask open ended questions, e.g. 'Why do you think the eggs are surrounded by the jelly then?' and 'Why do you think the frog spawn needs to have flies to eat?'

▶ Help children to make links with earlier experiences, e.g 'So you had spawn in your grandad's pond, and then they changed into newts?'

## Another great idea:

▶ If you have access to an incubator (you might be able to borrow one from a local nature reserve), then hatch some duck eggs with the children – it is a good idea to locally source partially incubated eggs as these will hatch withinin a few days, alternatively use a national source e.g. www.happychickcompany.co.uk).

▶ Explain to children how to care for the eggs – the incubator is needed to keep the eggs warm, then the heated light will keep the newly hatched ducklings warm.

▶ Ducklings grow from fluffy ducklings to fully feathered adults in around six weeks. Discuss the process with children and record their comments.

# Beautiful beanstalks

This practical experience uses a popular story to teach children more about planting and growing.

## Focus:

Talking about change and how to care for living things.

## What you could provide:

▶ Biodegradable flower pots, watering cans and potting compost

▶ Runner beans

▶ Magnifying glasses

▶ Some informative text about runner beans

▶ A copy of *Jack and the Beanstalk* (preferably an illustrated version)

# What you could do:

▶ Ensure children are familiar with the story of *Jack and the Beanstalk*.

▶ Investigate the runner beans together, using the magnifying glasses – point out colours, texture and the smell of the beans, as well as any similarities and differences between beans.

▶ Using compost, help the children to plant the beans in the pots.

▶ Water the beans each day with the children.

▶ Once the beanstalks have grown to about 10 centimetres tall, plant in a vegetable plot outdoors. If you don't have access to a vegetable plot in your setting, you could set up an area for growbags with the children.

## What you could say:

▶ Talk to the children about what is needed for the beans to grow into healthy plants, e.g. 'How much compost do you think we need?' and 'How many beans should we put in each pot?'

▶ Encourage children to think about how to care for the plants, and discuss this, e.g. 'How will we remember to water the beans every day? or 'How do we make sure they aren't over-watered?'

▶ As the beans begin to sprout, measure how tall they are with the children.

▶ Engage children who notice and talk about changes to the plants – the first buds, flowers and tiny beans forming.

▶ Point out the insects that visit the plants.

## Another great idea:

▶ When the beans are fully grown, harvest them together.

▶ Talk to the children about the space and size of the beans.

▶ Make a bean salad together – if you have one, you could use other salad vegetables that grow in your vegetable plot.

▶ Discuss the flavours of the bean salad, prompting children to make comparisons and links with meals they eat at home.

# Parachute fun

This lively group activity encourages children to run around, shout out loud and practice gross motor skills through arm movements.

## Focus:

Working with other children; addressing each other by name.

## What you could provide:

▶ A small parachute, or a colourful duvet cover or soft shower curtain

▶ You will need at least one other adult to help you

## What you could do:

▶ With a small group of children, hold the edges of the parachute and gently move it up and down together. Continue until you have a good rhythm.

▶ As you move the parachute, children take turns to each call out their name.

▶ Once you establish a slow, steady rhythm, you call out a child's name. The child must run under the parachute as the others continue to move it up and down. When they return to the circle, that child calls out the name of another child. The next child does the same, calling out a different name and so on.

## What you could say:

▶ Talk to the children about 'rhythm', using appropriate vocabulary including 'up' and 'down'.

▶ Prompt children to remember the names of the other children in the group.

## Another great idea:

▶ Play the parachute game 'Fruit Salad' with a larger group of children (you will need at least three adults to help you).

▶ Verbally list fruits together, e.g. strawberry, pear, orange, apple, plum.

▶ Each child must choose a fruit that they want to 'be'. Ask them to take it in turns to tell the rest of the group which fruit they have chosen.

▶ Once you have established a steady up and down parachute movement, call out the name of one fruit ,e.g. 'strawberry'. Each child who has chosen 'strawberry' runs under the parachute and swaps places with another 'strawberry' child. Continue until all the children have had several turns changing places.

▶ At intervals, call 'fruit salad' – this means that all the children must swap places, while the adults hold up the parachute.

# Further reading and resources

Biemiller, A. (2003) 'Vocabulary: needed if more children are to read well.' Reading Psychology, 24:323-335

Bromley, H. (2004) *50 Exciting ideas for Storyboxes*. Cambridge: Lawrence Education

DCSF (2008-2010) 'Every Child a Talker : Guidance for Early Language Lead Practitioners', www.foundationyears.org.uk/2011/10/every-child-a-talker-guidance-for-early-language-lead-practitioners/ [accessed March 2016]

DCSF (2008-2010) 'Every Child a Talker : Guidance for Early Language Consultants',www.foundationyears.org.uk/files/2011/10/EveryChild_a_Talker_consultants_guidance11.pdf [accessed March 2016]

Dockrell, J., Stuart, M. & King, D. (2006) 'Supporting oral language skills in the early years'. Literacy Today.

Goswami, U. And Bryant, P. (1990) *Phonological Skills and Learning to Read*. Hove: Lawrence Earlbaum Associates

Hart, B. & Risley, T. R. (1995). *Meaningful Differences in the Everyday Experience of Young American Children*. Baltimore: Paul H. Brookes Publishing Co.

Jones, M (2015) *Talking and Learning with Young Children*. London: Sage

Maclean, M., Bryant, P., and Bradley, L. (1987) 'Rhymes, Nursery Rhymes, and Reading in Early Childhood'. Merrill-Palmer Quarterly, 33(3) 255-281

Stevens, J (2011) 'Let's Talk! About young children's communication and language development', EYE Volume 13 No 4 August 2011

Stevens, J (2012) *Planning for the Early Years – Storytelling and Storymaking*, Bournemouth: Practical Preschool

Wasik, B.A., Bond, M.A. & Hindman, A. (2006) 'The effects of a language and literacy intervention on head start children and teachers'. Journal of Educational Psychology, 98, 63-74.

Whitehurst, G.J., Arnold, D., Epstein, J.N., Angell, A.L., Smith, M. & Fischel, J.E. (1998) 'A picture book reading intervention in day care and home for children from low-income families', Developmental Psychology, 30, pp.679-689.

# Useful websites

Core books and materials about reading: www.clpe.org.uk

High quality, durable, wooden play resources: www.communityplaythings.co.uk

Outdoor resources and materials for den making: www.cosydirect.com

Fertilised eggs for hatching: www.happychickcompany.co.uk

BookStart survey summary: http://education.scholastic.co.uk/content/8817

# The **Little Books** series consists of:

50
All through the year
Bags, Boxes & Trays
Big Projects
Bricks & Boxes
Building Vocabulary
Celebrations
Christmas
Circle Time
Clay and Malleable Materials
Clothes and Fabric
Colour, Shape and Number
Cooking from Stories
Cooking Together
Counting
Dance
Dens
Discovery Bottles
Dough
Drama and Performance
Explorations
Fine Motor Skills
Free and Found
Fun on a Shoestring
Games with Sounds
Gross Motor Skills
Growing Things
Healthy Eating
ICT
Investigations
Junk Music
Kitchen Stuff

Language Fun
Light and Shadow
Listening
Living Things
Look and Listen
Making Books and Cards
Mark Making
Maths Activities
Maths from Stories
Maths Outdoors
Maths Problem Solving
Maths Songs and Games
Measures
Messy Play
Minibeast Hotels
Multi-sensory Stories
Music and Movement
My Neighbourhood
Numbers
Nursery Rhymes
Opposites
Outdoor Play
Outside in All Weathers
Painting
Parachute Play
Persona Dolls
Phonics
Playground Games
Print Making
Props for Writing
Puppets in Stories
Resistant Materials

Rhythm and Raps
Role Play
Role Play Windows
Sand and Water
Science through Art
Scissor Skills
Seasons
Sequencing Skills
Sewing and Weaving
Shape and Space
Small World Play
Sound Ideas
Special Days
Stories from around the world
Story bags
Storyboards
Storybuilding
Storytelling
Team Games
Time and Money
Time and Place
Topsy Turvy
Traditional Tales
Treasure Baskets
Treasure Boxes
Tuff Spot Activities
Washing lines
Woodland Challenges
Woodwork
Writing

All available from
## www.bloomsbury.com/featherstone

If you have found this book useful you might also like ...

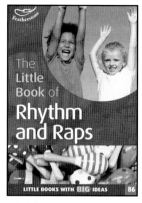

**LB Rhythm and Raps**
ISBN 978-1-4729-0256-6

**LB Building Vocabulary**
ISBN 978-1-4729-1855-0

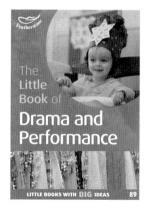

**LB Drama and Performance**
ISBN 978-1-4729-0949-7

**LB Music and Movement**
ISBN 978-1-4729-1272-5

All available from

**www.bloomsbury.com/featherstone**